More

MW00480403

99 Way. ~~ ᴍᴀᴋᴇ a
Flight Attendant Fly—
Off the Handle!

Whether you fly once a year or 60,000 miles a year as I do, you'll enjoy Deveny's *99 Ways to Make a Flight Attendant Fly—Off the Handle!* The suggestions and vignettes in this book are logical and realistic. The way they are presented kept me laughing from the beginning to the end. This is the perfect gift for the traveler in your life!

--Andrea Sisco, Armchair Interviews Host

While giving useful insights into how to make a flight attendant's job more difficult or more agreeable, at the same time 99 Ways makes for some hilarious light reading.

—Bill Leader, Editor of DFW People Newspaper

. . . a very true and revealing look into the experiences of flight attendants. *99 Ways to Make a Flight Attendant Fly— Off the Handle!* is right on the mark. A must read for both airline employees and especially the flying public. (Refer to Offenses 76 and 99.) Thank you, JoAnn!

—Timothy Sneer, 30-year flight attendant

This book is an absolute gift for either the novice or the road warrior traveler. As a constant and surly frequent flyer myself, I didn't realize how little I could do to make my airtime so much more pleasant. Deveny makes it fun for me to see all my sins!

—Jean Mork Bredeson, General Manager, Service 800

Love this book! We all step out of line on flights and this book will help you appreciate what flight attendants put up with . . . us! Grab your ticket, board the plane and fasten your seat belt and behave. Here's some sensible advice from flight attendants to help you enjoy your flight (and theirs too) by not getting on their nerves.

—*Chris Sellick, Australia*

Quite frankly . . . I'm a flight attendant. I received this book from a co-worker for my birthday. It made me chuckle so much. Why? Because we keep reading them out loud and yelling "That's SO true!!! If you really want to know what not to do on an airplane, this is the book for you. All the missteps are presented in a witty and entertaining format that definitely relates WHY things are annoying to us.

—*A.D. Eads, Richmond, Virginia*

This book should be read and followed by all travelers. Ms. Deveny presents airline etiquette in a very humorous way. It is easily read and will bring many smiles to your face and maybe even an occasional chuckle. Read it and learn ways to impress your flight attendants and fellow passengers!

—*Reading in Seattle*

99 Ways to Make a Flight Attendant Fly— Off the Handle!

A GUIDE FOR THE NOVICE OR OBLIVIOUS AIR TRAVELER

JoAnn Kuzma Deveny

Fly High Books

Other books by JoAnn Kuzma Deveny

When Bluebirds Fly:
Losing a Child, Living with Hope

I Am Widow, Hear Me Roar:
Confessions of a Surviving Spouse

99 Ways to Make a Flight Attendant Fly— Off the Handle!

A GUIDE FOR THE NOVICE OR OBLIVIOUS AIR TRAVELER

JoAnn Kuzma Deveny

2018
Fly High Books
Mound, MN

Fly High Books
5017 Wilshire Blvd.
Mound, MN 55364

ISBN 13: 978-0-578-41584-0
Library of Congress Catalog Number: 2018913392

Illustrated by: Richard Carl Lehman

Cover design
James Monroe Design LLC.

Printed in the United States of America

2nd Edition, 2018

1. Air travel—Humor--Advice 2. Flight attendant—Humor
3. Aviation—Humor 4. Airline-Humor

To order an autographed copy visit:
www.JoAnnDeveny.com

*Dedicated to the crew members who perished
on September 11, 2001*

Good day, ladies and gentlemen.

Good day, ladies and gentlemen. I would like to welcome you onboard *99 Ways to Make a Flight Attendant Fly—Off the Handle!* Our approximate reading time is one hour and twelve minutes. The opinions of this book are under the command of the author and she has predicted only minor turbulence along the way to our destination.

Please stow all your "extra" baggage in the overhead bin or underneath the seat in front of you. We ask that you take your assigned easy chair, fasten your seat belt, and don your reading glasses in preparation for page two. At this time, you will need to turn off and stow all electrifying opinions for the duration of the book.

Once we are airborne, you may recline your seat-back, relax, and enjoy the viewpoint.

We hope you enjoy your literary journey.

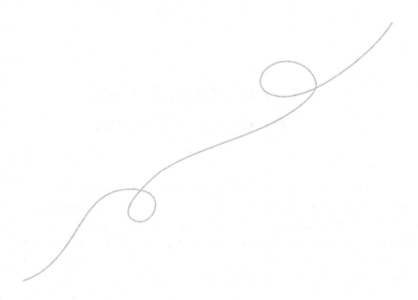

Take Off...

Oh, the mysteries of air travel!

The rush of adrenalin and a stature of command overtake us when the wheels of our plane lift from the solid ground of the tarmac and we leave the gravity of Mother Earth. While we soar through the vacant stratosphere, with clouds as our equals and snow-capped mountaintops far below us, we ponder the ambiguity of eternity. A feeling of superiority overcomes us as we embrace autonomy and gaze into the infinite skies surrounding us.

Then we turn from the window to merely find ourselves sandwiched between the likes of Hulk Hogan or Mama Cass—confined within a circular tube for the next three hours.

There was a time (at my airline interview 40 years ago) when I "loved to travel" and "loved people." After approximately 16,640 flights, 8,320 "Bah-bye nows", and 661,600 pop tabs pulled. I don't care much for travel and have also left behind my passion for the latter. Don't get me wrong, I still appreciate my "passenger" in singular form. It's the *plural* that gets to me at times.

Since the other day—when my coffeepot spilled onto a businessman's laptop after I tripped over a screaming toddler who was crawling through the aisle of a 737—I've been feeling a desperate need to organize my work environment.

There are guidebooks written for nearly every circumstance of life. Never having embraced rules as a youngster, it now seems odd that I would impose my policies on someone else. But after nearly 40 years of "stew" hours under my belt and approximately 157 spilled coffee-pots, I've come to recognize the necessity for educating the masses on the art of effective air travel. As should be expected, flight attendants are bombarded with numerous memos, e-mails, and training sessions on how to serve their passengers better. Yet, there is no information available for our *passengers* on how to behave so their flight attendants *can* serve them better.

Also, flight attendants are the sounding boards of passenger complaints. We've stoically maintained our com-posure while being repetitively and emotionally battered by passenger grievances throughout the years. So, I believe it's time for a flight attendant's viewpoint.

Throughout this text I will use the pronouns "she" and "her" when referring to the flight attendants, partly for convenience, and partly because there are still more females than males in the industry (5:1). To give men an equal billing, I will refer to the businessman versus businesswoman throughout my narration and chance being politically incorrect. But mind you, I would *never* insinuate that men are the more obvious transgressors regarding my 99 irritations (now trying to be politically correct).

When referring to an aircraft in terms of flight crew, passenger count, and seating arrangement, I will use the 757-5500 aircraft model as a standard example. Unfor-tunately, this is the aircraft I am most familiar with. Because airline crews speak in a different dialect than the more grounded populace, a glossary is in the back of this book to help define some basic airline terms.

Even though you may find yourself enjoying the next few pages, this book was not solely written for entertainment purposes. Along with your boarding pass, this guidebook is a necessity for every passenger before boarding an airplane. It is the bible of air travel. Besides, you too may become irritated by an oblivious fellow passenger and could personally benefit by passing a copy on to them.

If you see yourself in the next few pages, please don't be offended—you are not alone. If you feel that my requests are trite, please take this as an indication that I've covered all the bases. It may be hard to believe that flight attendants, in a perfect world, are patient people. Supposedly, we were hired for that trait. Yet all our composure can change, as you may know, when 57 passengers commit one offense in my book or one passenger commits 57. It's the *accumulation* that can send us to that "stew" breaking point. At which time we will try to regroup in the galley and vent—or at times, grab a beer and blow a chute. This is referred to as "doing a Slater." (Refer to **Steve Slater** in the glossary).

If you think that some flight attendants have inadequate skills in customer service, you are correct, there may be a few. But then, I encourage you to write a book titled *99 Ways to Make a Passenger Fly out the Window? (oops)—Off the Handle!* I would love to read it; I'm always open to improvement.

However, if you are one of my favorite customers— one of those who can take life with a grain of salt, roll with the punches, be enlightened by a little constructive criticism, and easily laugh at themselves—prepare yourself for takeoff!

01

Believe that a reservation guarantees you a seat on an airplane

Don't be a procrastinator, it will not be to your advantage. You'll need to check in at least 60 minutes before a domestic flight and two hours before an international flight. Inside of these time parameters, your seat may be legally auctioned to the highest bidder. Or better yet, check in on your computer at home 24 hours beforehand.

And don't forget those security lines. It may take over an hour just to get to the formidable "NAKED MACHINE". There you will stand in surrender position and envision a pimpled-face teenager in front of a screen in a back room holding a porn magazine. Which I'm sure is not the case, but it may come to mind unwarranted.

Many flight crews opt for a pat-down versus the scan, mainly because we may need to go through security approximately 157 times a year and prefer not to risk a miscalculation on the proposed radiation that these machines emit. I understand that some people are offended by the pat-down experience, but please don't take it out on your TSA (refer to glossary), they're just doing their job.

Some say that if the TSAs did their job any better, we would expect a nice dinner afterwards. Personally, being single and not extremely modest, I don't mind an evasive pat-down on occasion.

02

Board the airplane hungry

If you need to leave home at 6 a.m. to catch a 10 a.m. flight, it would be wise to feed your kids *before* you get on the aircraft. There may be 148 passengers to be served and only two flight attendants to get the job done. You may be looking at a possible one-hour wait after boarding before you see any morsel of nutrition; two hours if you're seated in the back row. This is the best-case scenario when your flight is actually scheduled for a meal. (More commonly, we will be selling preservative-based morsels which have the consistency of cardboard. Even more surprising, we often run out of these little gems half way through the service.)

Now, if there's a mechanical problem or weather delay, or if you find yourself stuck in the middle of airport morning rush hour, you could merely be anticipating breakfast on an afternoon flight.

If you don't have time to eat before a flight, I would suggest bringing your own food rations onboard...while keeping your fellow passengers in mind. There's a reason why stinky tofu and rotten Korean skate fish got their name.

Speaking of odors, always remember that morning shower of soap and water and try to resist that morning shower of your favorite perfume or cologne before a flight.

03

Don't know the FARs

It can be an awkward moment when your flight attendant sternly fixates her gaze on you and spits out that infamous statement: "Sir, it's against the *FARs!*" What in the heck are FARs, you ask?

They are *Federal Aviation Regulations:* rules set by the Federal Aviation Administration, that are enforced by your crew members. Refusal to abide by them can lead to a hefty fine, ejection from the flight, federal prosecution, and/or imprisonment. So, pay attention; ignorance will not be accepted as an excuse. Here are a few basic FARs every passenger should know. For example:

FAR 121.580: Do not assault, threaten, intimidate, or interfere with a crew member.

FAR 121.589: Bags cannot be blocking any aisle way or emergency exit and must be stowed in closed overhead bins or underneath a seat.

FAR 121.317(f): Keep seat belt fastened when seat belt light is on. (The most difficult rule for passengers to abide by.)

FAR 121.317(k): Comply with crew member instructions. (My favorite.)

04

Come unprepared

FYI: We typically do not have a refrigerator to chill your medicine or a microwave to heat the baby's bottle. If you are diabetic, bring a snack. If you have a child, bring snacks, diapers, formula, games, movies, puzzles, coloring books... you get the gist. If you require a flight attendant's undivided attention and the inventory of a drug store, bring along a *personal* attendant.

05

If you plan on happy hour, don't bring a credit card

Now I'm going to age myself.

When graduating from "stew" school, I was issued a cockpit key, regulations manual, FAA approved identification badge and a roll of quarters. At that time, I didn't understand the significance of that wad of change but soon found out that it was routine for passengers to use a $5 bill for a 50-cent beer. Yes, that was the price for a brewski. Because most of us spent that generous gift of change before our first flight, we regretfully discovered that there was no cash register in the galley and the closest bank was the captain's billfold.

Now that we have stepped out of the Stone Age, your Abe Lincoln probably isn't good anymore. Most airlines only accept plastic. On the other hand, your flight attendants are not as particular. While appreciating the convenience of our credit card readers, at the same time, we wish that these devices included a tip application.

Here's where your Abe may come in handy.

06

Board the airplane intoxicated

I've always believed that if every flight attendant at my company were issued a shot of whiskey before each flight, her disposition would greatly improve and ours would be the airline of preference. But because your flight attendants are, hopefully, cold-stone sober (one of the FARs), we can easily identify the passengers who are not (another FAR).

Even if you are on a flight to Las Vegas or Cancun, intoxication is not an excuse for being obnoxious or loud and can lead to ejection from a flight—preferably at the gate of departure.

So, I wouldn't bother saying good-bye to that airport bartender you've befriended while drinking the last of your five drafts; you'll be seeing him sooner than you think.

Please take note, only alcohol served by your flight attendants can be consumed on board the aircraft. Mixing your own drinks is the same premise as bringing your own whiskey into McDonalds to mix with your slushy. No and no.

07

Ask for two predeparture drinks

This is the typical scenario while we are boarding an aircraft.

The lead flight attendant and her 3 coworkers greet and scrutinize 170 boarding passengers, check emergency equipment and catering supplies, fill ice buckets, prepare the galley for inflight service, ensure that 80 bins are closed and that 14 able-bodied people (ABPs) at the emergency exits are briefed, make several announcements, and hang 22 coats.

That's our workload if everything goes as planned— which it never does. Then there are a few more things we do: check bags, be briefed by a late captain, serve drinks to the cockpit, call catering for missing supplies, resolve a dupe seat assignment, move exit row peeps, fill pillow and blanket requests, and trouble-shoot the numerous questions posed by passengers.

Besides these duties, the airlines have deemed it necessary that we serve 22 first-class beverages against the flow of boarding passengers passing through the same two-foot aisle. You only need to imagine a salmon swimming upstream.

Say I'm wrong, but should it ever be necessary for a person to down *two* scotch and waters during this time? I don't know why these beverages are called what they are. Rarely is there time to drink one *pre*departure, let alone two.

O8

Don't dress for the occasion

Some retired flight attendants remember the days before deregulation when every passenger wore formal attire on an airplane. Some miss that era. I, on the other hand, don't take offense to passengers being comfortable while traveling...as long as they remember sanitation. For instance, no one fancies sitting next to a broad-chested, sweaty guy wearing a muscle shirt that reveals his armpit hair. And if you prefer wearing sandals, please leave your feet on the floor (not on the tray table next to you), and don't pick the flight between Memphis and Chicago to cut your toenails. It's been done.

Many of our aircraft have sensitive heating systems and many of your flight attendants are experiencing inflight hot flashes (refer to Offense 35), the temperature on flights may be cooler than you would prefer. Wear long pants, bring a sweater, and grab a blanket during boarding *before* you sit down. Or better yet don't: those blankets don't get cleaned very often and there is usually a shortage. You might prefer to bring your own layers.

I believe that some passengers' brain cells must rust in the humidity of a Miami hotel room when dressing for the flight back to a northern destination. Even though they've lived in the tundra all their lives, it temporarily slips their minds that they usually wear *pants* in Minnesota in January.

Flight attendants will forever be puzzled by passengers, wearing the same sandals, tank top, and Bermuda shorts that they wore in the Bahamas, exiting the aircraft onto a Minneapolis jetway and exclaiming with amazement how cold it is.

09

Don't bring treats for your flight attendants

Even though it seldom occurs, bribery is not out of the question. It may have been three days since anything other than airplane food has touched our lips. For one hermetically sealed box of treats, we will be indebted to you for the rest of your life or the duration of the flight (whichever is shorter).

10

Block the aisle during boarding

It is wise to proactively use the bathroom in the airport before boarding and to remove your electronic devices from your bag before you place it in the overhead bin. Once you're seated, please remain seated. Departure times are very sensitive to human nature, and delays will occur when 57 passengers forget to plan ahead before boarding.

Did I say that men were *not* the more obvious transgressors to the 99 ways? Okay, except for this one thing.

When you stand in the aisle folding four layers of outer garments with the precision of an American soldier folding Old Glory, and then proceed to methodically lay them one...after...another...in the overhead bin—are you aware of the 157 people waiting behind you?

11

Be demanding as soon as you set foot on the airplane

Once upon a time on a flight to Philadelphia, there was a surly businessman who decided to have a "chat" with the pilots during their predeparture checklist. This passenger decided to unload all his weekly frustrations through the door of the cockpit soon after boarding the aircraft. The captain, usually a diplomatic man, turned around from his job with a smile.

"There you are! I've been looking all over for you," he exclaimed in a most pleasant voice. "We always have one idiot on every flight, and now I know where you are!" Pilots, overall, do not have as much experience or patience for handling deviant behavior as flight attendants do.

When a passenger starts out being demanding or rude, chances are he or she will maintain character throughout the flight. If you are that one, you will be pegged by your flight attendants as the "Needy" passenger and be the brunt of galley prattle for the next three hours. It will be as if you had the big scarlet letter "N" imprinted on your chest.

12

Ask a flight attendant to stow your luggage

We are required to wear nylons, pumps, and dresses. If our job description was to stow every passenger's fifty-pound bag in the overhead bin, we would have been issued back braces with our boarding hats.

There are two things we can usually do for you—we can help you find an open space for your bag or we can gate-check it. Gate-checking allows you to check last minute bags at the gate of departure or at the doorway of the aircraft. This is a very convenient service and makes it *almost* impossible for the ramp rats (refer to glossary) to load your luggage on the wrong airplane.

But be aware that gate-checking may mean retrieving your bags at baggage claim, not at planeside. Also, what some frequent flyers already know, and use to their advantage, this service is usually free. I must admit that avoiding the checked-baggage fee is attractive, but this new budgeting tactic could ultimately lead to extra carry-on bags and a late flight. That would be *your* late flight and possibly *your* missed connection.

13

Believe that bulkhead seats are exempt from bag stowage rules

You may be inwardly gloating while enjoying the ample legroom at your front row seat that faces a wall. And you may be pitying the poor six-foot-four guy seated behind you who has his knees caressing his chin. What you may not realize is that when you're in a bulkhead seat, there is no such thing as "underneath the seat in front of you". Don't try squeezing your bag behind your legs—we caught on to that one years ago. All your bags need to be stowed in an overhead bin.

Remember, loose newspapers, magazines, purses, pop cans, dirty plates, and your size twelve shoes are not exceptions to the FAR that requires a clear aisleway. I imagine that a stray *Wall Street Journal* would act much like a banana peel during an evacuation.

14

Believe that you bought an overhead bin with your ticket

If you're reading your magazine during boarding with your bags still sitting in the aisle, don't act as if I'm intruding when I remind you of the fact. *I am doing you a favor*. Overhead space is limited.

I once had two first-class "gentlemen" physically fight over the overhead bin above their heads. You may have noticed that there is not one bin per passenger on any aircraft (refer to Offense 29). Remember, you have been assigned a seat, not a bin.

Refer to the adage "First come—First served." It pertains to many circumstances in life.

15

Board the aircraft with three bags and the kitchen sink

Normally, you are allowed one carry-on bag, 9×14×22-inch or smaller (overstuffed garment bags are not exempt from this rule), and one briefcase or purse, preferably much smaller than these dimensions. Luggage should be less than approximately 30 pounds (check with your airline—and this includes purses). Canes and walkers can be accommodated. Children's strollers and car seats can be gate-checked and retrieved by the door of the aircraft at arrival—which is more convenient for you than trying to stow them while your arms are full of screaming munchkins.

I guarantee that whatever your domestic destination, you can buy a stereo speaker, cooler, flower pot, couch cushion, or toaster oven there that is identical to the one you just dragged onto my airplane.

And the answer to your question is "yes." On one flight I *did* have a passenger bring on a kitchen sink.

16

Don't stow your bag properly

When your chin is resting on both your knees, that is an indication that your roll-a-bag under the seat in front of you is sticking into the aisle a bit too far. Also remember that the phone-booth craze of the fifties is long gone, so let's not try to break the record for the number of bags one can fit in an overhead bin. And please don't leave your 24-inch bag in the 21-inch bin without testing to see if the door shuts.

Although it's not your fault that a six-foot seven man probably designed the middle bins on a 767, it would be very considerate if you closed the bin that you were just able to open. Even at five-foot-seven, neither can I bench press 150 pounds nor reach that overhead bin without standing on *your* assigned seat with the sticky, soda-saturated soles of my inflight shoes.

17

Refuse to check your luggage

"But I *can't* check *my* bag!" We've heard this many times.

Only two choices here: (a) you can check your bag or (b) stay behind with it. Because we do not have one overhead bin per passenger, when you board a full flight within the last ten minutes before departure, you may need to check your only bag.

I know life is not fair when the first 100 passengers are allowed to bring their bags onboard, and yours must be checked. But that doesn't change the fact that there is no "secret" stowage area in the galley nor can we miraculously create an empty bin by waving a magic stew wand. Oh, what I could do with that wand! (Refer to Offense 73.)

FYI: The overhead bins haven't gotten smaller over the years (the aircraft is probably older than your pilots)—your bag has gotten bigger. Don't ever believe that luggage salesman when he assures you that the $300 hope-chest-on-wheels he is trying to sell you will fit on any aircraft.

18

Expect to hang a garment bag in a coat closet

One may find large closets on some of the older airplanes, which were built at a time when garment bags were made of thin nylon and designed to hold one dress suit. If you bring one of those relics, your flight attendants will more likely try to accommodate it.

Now that luggage companies are merely attaching hangers onto folding roll-a-bags, many airplane manufacturers and airlines have diminished the size of closets on newer airplanes—usually to add more seats. Though, they may have finally realized what flight attendants have known all along— that a closet on an airplane merely makes the first five passengers happy and, once full, irritates the last 57.

19

Send your six-year-old on a flight by himself

Even though flight attendants try to be watchful of every unaccompanied minor, once again, there's that 148-passenger factor that comes into play. Your child will never be monitored as well as he or she deserves. That guy with the blue hair and nose ring seated next to your daughter may look like the Smurf in her coloring book, but he could have a dark side. The airlines do not screen their passengers with psychological tests.

And sometimes it's not just a matter of depositing your child at the gate and receiving him or her at the other end. Cancellations, misconnections, and airplane diversions do happen. If an adult gets bent out of shape by an unexpected layover in a strange city, how do you think a child would feel?

Make sure your child is old enough to handle all these situations. If this be your only guideline—most flight attendants wouldn't send their own children alone on an airplane until they're well into their teens.

While FAs can easily be distinguished from passengers by that hardened, vacant gaze in their eyes when in the vicinity of their workplace, be assured we do cry. And nothing makes us more teary-eyed than when we are trying to comfort a distraught young child who is leaving his mother or father for the summer.

Most of our unaccompanied minors are the products of a divorce in which one parent lives cross country from the other. Sell the Porsche and buy a ticket to fly with him. Or better yet, parents, move closer to one another. He'll be 18 before you know it.

20

Be clueless to electronic device regulations

Okay, this one we deserve. The rules for battery operated toys seem to change more times than Liz Taylor has planned weddings and more times than I've had to update this chapter.

But when I inform a passenger of an infraction and he says, "I know," while continuing to ignore me, that translates as "I don't care" or "Talk to the hand." I've gained much insight into the hidden interpretations of a human mind from raising a teenager.

Definition of an electronic device: Anything that runs on a battery and can be turned off. And no, your husband's pacemaker should not be turned off no matter how much life insurance is involved. Honestly, I have been asked this.

21

Use the bathroom while we are taxiing

Taxiing times can be trying when lengthy, especially for that 6-year old traveling by himself. But if you feel a bursting desire to use our facilities during taxiing, please understand that if you do so, we can't move the aircraft. Because you are not in your seat belted, we will need to stop taxiing, lose our place in line, and possibly wait *another* hour before take-off. I don't think your fellow passengers would like that. At that time, the lead flight attendant may become a tad more specific with her announcements.

"Ladies and gentlemen, if the gentleman in the yellow sweater in the aft lavatory does not take his *assigned* seat, we will consequently return to number 23 in line for take-off."

It's amazing what a little peer pressure can do.

22

Ask to be seated in first class

I could make a handsome profit if granted the power to award that vacant first-class seat to the highest bidder. Most airlines astutely leave that job to the gate agents or reservations whom you deal with before boarding the aircraft. Unless you are George Clooney, your being handsome and turning on the charm will not influence me. I do have my standards.

If you are a family of four and have only one first-class seat, please don't play musical chairs between sections. I know that it is family budgeting at its finest if dad has the cocktail before dinner, mom replaces him to dine on the salad, junior sends mom back so he can relish the steak, and then sister quietly slips in to finish off the desert. I've honestly witnessed this scenario more than once. Please pick your seat and stay in it—we are easily confused.

Some people pay a large fee to be "upgraded." But in most cases, our valuable frequent-flyers are granted that seat in a hierarchy determined by the number of airline meals they've had to consume in one year. And my frequent-flyers always know their rank: "But I'm a *silver* card member!" (equivalent to 52 smoked turkey sandwiches eaten); "But I'm a *platinum* card member!" (131 smoked turkey sandwiches).

What they don't know is that, from top echelon, there are probably 9 platinum, 20 gold, 40 silver, and 70 preferred frequent-flyers on board, all vying for that last first-class seat.

Hmmm. I could make a handsome profit, couldn't I?

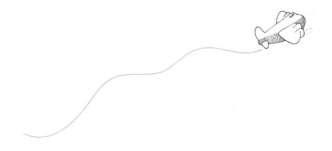

23

Refuse to follow crew instructions

Even though this refers to my favorite FAR, flight attendants usually don't abuse this bestowed power. Although I have known a few flight attendants who enjoy ordering Mr. Businessman around, most of us do not get our kicks out of telling people what to do. *It's our job.*

Any flight attendant will tell you that getting passengers aboard the aircraft is the most difficult segment of their workday (though, oddly enough, it's the part we don't get paid for).

So be cooperative, please. Actually, the concept is pretty basic—you board, stow your bag, sit down, and fasten your seat belt. Most of my breath is depleted reminding passengers of those four simple concepts. Half of them just plain ignore me (Offense 42), and the other half must have checked their brains with their luggage. You may also find the latter in the airport either *standing* on the "walk" side of a moving sidewalk or stopping at the end of an escalator while a pile of air travelers imitate dominos behind them.

I know generalizations and stereotyping are not politically correct. But when several flight attendants avoid a certain route, there must be a consistent factor involved. I understand that the United States has as many differing cultures as Europe does, and that a flight attendant from Mole Hill, Idaho, may not relate well to her Miami passengers. Any displaced Southerner who has been deposited north of the Mason– Dixon Line will understand what I am talking about.

Although I'm a Midwesterner, I honestly enjoy New Yorkers—most of the time. Because they have a refreshing forthright approach and don't beat around the bush, there are no hidden agendas with these folks. Also, I have experienced some extraordinary acts of kindness among Big Apple passengers. Yet I can guarantee that no matter what a flight attendant announces on a New York flight, the opposite will be done. Cell phones won't be in airplane mode (Offense 20); luggage will be blocking the emergency exits (Offense 13); and passengers will stand when they're told to sit (Offense 66). When the flight attendants say "black" the passengers will say "white." I'm sure not all New Yorkers are guilty of this, but I've found 57 percent of 180 is still a little overwhelming.

Maybe it is because of their fine city's large population that New Yorkers strive to be individuals. Possibly they need to stand out in a crowd so not to be another inconsequential human among the masses? Educate me, New Yorkers!

24

Blame us for the weather

Even though the airline management would like to believe they have the powers of God, and some pilots think that they *are* God, we cannot control the thunderstorm that is delaying your flight. If you derive pleasure from flying through thunder clouds and lightening, join the Air Force.

I am comforted by the fact that our air traffic controllers are usually attentive, and our pilots are usually chicken. Trust me, the last thing we want is a kamikaze captain who needs to prove his manhood by frolicking through a tornado.

25

Try to obtain anything that is free

Once there was an elderly gentleman whose doctor strongly recommended that he use oxygen while flying. But, alas, every time he traveled, he would ring his call button to summon the FA and announce that he was having difficulties breathing. All this to avoid the fee for a preordered bottle and use our onboard emergency oxygen for free. Now, case in point, this guy had emphysema, asthma, and only one lung! He wins the runner-up prize in my logbook for the thriftiest air traveler. (The winner is any parent who pretends their child is under two-years-old, so the child may fly free by sitting in the parent's lap, unsafely, without a seat belt.)

Then there are some passengers who get a charge out of accumulating *anything* that is complimentary, whether they need it or not. Next time you request two cans of soda, a cup of coffee, and a carton of milk when the beverage cart comes around, ask yourself, "Am I really going to drink all of this on a 45-minute flight?" If the answer is "yes," then ask yourself, "How many trips to the bathroom can I accomplish during that time?"

Another handy thing to know is that your flight attendant is not an office supply store. Even though there may be a favorite pen clipped to her uniform vest, she is not required to lend it to every passenger who forgets to bring their own.

Also, we flight attendants would like you to know that many domestic flights do not have playing cards anymore. Although we may have numerous personal items—blankets, reading lights, Band-Aids, nasal spray, aspirin, ibuprofen, pencils, plastic wings, Imodium tablets, beverages—we *do not* have playing cards.

26

Be arrogant

As flight attendants, we run into many famous celebrities, athletes, politicians, and royal figures on our flights. Many of us have become numbed to popularity and aren't readily awed by the stature of our passengers. Though, I admit that my heart rate would still increase if Mel Gibson walked by me in the Los Angeles airport again. And I would be pleased if Tim Allan, Margot Kidder, Gloria Steinem, Henry Winkler, Bruce Springsteen, Tara Lipinsky, Allan Richards, Dan Rather, Diane Keaton, and Tiny Tim (rest his soul and his ukulele) were on my airplane again. Those were all memorable flights. But the famous passenger I remember most was the Queen of Sweden.

One morning in 1989 before boarding (while I knelt on the dirty galley floor of the DC-9 with my head stuck inside a rancid cart as I searched for a missing meal), a manager from my airline appeared at the doorway. Adorned in an expensive business suit and assuming an air of importance, he informed me that the Queen of Sweden and ten of her escorting entourage were to be on my flight. He went into a lengthy oration on the protocol of addressing royalty. I was told never to speak to the Queen directly. She would have her "concierge" seated next to her, and I was *always* to go through him and refer to "Her Majesty" when inquiring about her needs.

As an American citizen, I thought the whole idea a little overdone, yet knew I could oblige for a flight of merely two hours. So, when "Her Majesty" was seated and pre-departure drinks were to be served, I approached the concierge seated next to her. I cooed in my most respectful flight attendant voice possible, "Sir, would Her Majesty like a beverage before departure?" Well, this royal employee vacantly looked up from his newspaper for a moment, shrugged his shoulders while thumbing in the queen's direction and said, "I dunno... why don't you ask her?"

From this experience, and many others, I have learned that most famous individuals are not haughty. Unfortunately, there are some celebrity-wannabes who are not so obliging.

We may be lowly *galley wenches, aisle hags, trolley dolls,* or *sky bags* and you may be a corporate executive, but we are still not impressed by arrogance. Besides, many of us have side jobs and hobbies that are more indicative of our abilities than serving soda pop to the masses. There are flight attendants who are lawyers, nurses, artists, entrepreneurs, actors, actresses, DJs, musicians, CPAs, and even writers. I could be the hygienist who scrapes your teeth, the nurse who sticks you with a needle, the lawyer who prosecutes you or, better yet, my husband could be your boss. With the camaraderie of approximately 98,700 flight attendants and the lightspeed global rumor mill we possess at the tip of our tongues, you're a little outnumbered.

Take a lesson from the Queen of Sweden.

27

Ask stupid questions

As my father always said, there are no stupid questions. But I guarantee that to those that are marginally idiotic, you'll always get an appropriate answer.

Actual dialogue:

Passenger (rings call button after we hit turbulence)— "What was that?"
Flight Attendant (deadpan)—"Turbulence."
Passenger (looking at FA slyly)—"Is that the pat answer you give to everyone?"
Flight Attendant (knowing she's met her match)— "Yes, sir. I was really lying. We actually just ran over a curb on our last turn." Or, "I'm sorry, I knew I couldn't fool you. That was really the captain hitting his head on the steering wheel after passing out. Don't worry, the lead flight attendant has the airplane under control."

Passenger (on a 45-minute flight)—"What's the movie?"
Flight Attendant "Gone with the Wind. Just open your window and you'll get the picture."

Passenger "Could you microwave my husband's pillow? It's quite cold."
Flight Attendant (speechless)

And no, your child will not be sucked through the toilet and into the stratosphere when it flushes. (I'm not making this up!)

In addition to stupid questions, there are stupid answers. FYI: "Would you like peanuts or pretzels, Ma'am?" is a multiple-choice, not a "yes" or "no", question.

28

Tell stupid jokes

I believe we've heard them all. "I want my eggs over easy." Ha, ha. "I'll have my steak medium rare." Ha, ha.

How is it possible that everyone tells the same ones? Is there a book out there titled *99 Jokes to Bore Your Flight Attendant*?

29

Believe that every airline and every aircraft is the same

"Well, it fit on my last flight!" (Different airplane.) "The last flight attendant let me do it!" (She was either incompetent or busy giving oxygen to the gentleman in Offense 25.) "Skyway has Coke!" (We have Pepsi products and they don't.) "Trans Global has champagne and caviar!" (You paid more for your ticket with them.)

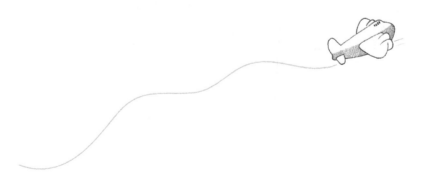

30

Make physical contact with a flight attendant

Molestation! Harassment! We have very little square footage during our 12-hour shift, and we take offense when someone invades the only personal space we have left—our own bodies.

A simple "Excuse me, ma'am" will get our attention. Don't poke us (we are not the Pillsbury doughboy) or pull on any of our body parts or clothing. In other words: *Don't touch our junk!*

If you do, you may find yourself at the end of a glare that could part the Red Sea

31

Sit in a flight attendant's jumpseat

Besides being against the formidable FARs, we are very possessive of our two-foot wide, fold-up board and what we have stored there. We have one seat to take in case we hit turbulence (or hit a curb, or the captain passes out).

In the same vein, for those who put their feet on the coffee table at home, please *do not* use the jumpseat for a footrest to elevate your stinky, shoeless feet. Heaven forbid the wrath of a stew!

Because of the added rows and reduced leg room on airplanes, I truly empathize with my passengers regarding their cramped quarters. But if you're seated in front of a jumpseat, please scoot those feet over to give us a little leg room, we won't be sitting for long.

With all the extra seats added to the airplanes, I'm surprised the airlines haven't vertically strapped the flight attendants, while standing up, to the inner fuselage like a fair ride. (Sorry, coworkers, you may eventually blame me for addressing this budgeting idea.)

32

Take a newspaper or magazine from our jumpseat or luggage

It's amazing how the possessions that were once ours suddenly become community property. I don't believe my jumpseat looks like a magazine rack. We seldom treat ourselves to a newspaper or scavenge the seats for a used one (with gum stuck in the corners and crosswords filled in).

My newspaper has been pilfered so many times that I now print my initials on the front page. After the crime, instead of fuming about it, I investigate the passengers who are indulging in that reading material.

Then when discovering my JD (or John Doe) in the corner, I transform into Ms. Hyde and proceed to deliver a hellacious lecture on the evils of stealing that even my son would make my son cringe.

33

Be impatient

Patience is an essential trait for any air traveler, especially if you're seated in back of the aircraft and the beverage carts start at the front. Yet sometimes, to confuse you, we will start at each end and serve the middle rows last. This method is aptly called "the squeeze." If you're seated in that midsection and are observant, you will see just that when we arrive at your row.

Overall, flight attendants usually hurry through the service to lengthen their leisure time afterward. We do not pause in the middle of our service for a "union break" unless there is severe turbulence. Trust me, we are doing the best we can with a standard of two servers and 148 people to feed. You try that at home with the kitchen the size of a closet.

Also, it's not necessary for you to know our arrival gate before we get there. First, the gate number will inevitably change once we land, and second, the suspense won't kill you (though our meals might).

34

Complain that you waited too long for service and then be unable to decide what you want

Enough said.

35

Tell a flight attendant she looks tired

If you are an avid flyer and haven't had your nose buried in a newspaper for 20 years, you may have noticed that your flight attendants are getting older. Unless we have a "sugar daddy" husband, our retirement usually starts when social security does and, even then, the funds are inadequate to pay a mortgage. I guess the airlines must want us to hang (pardon the pun) around until we need to peer over trifocal lenses to maneuver our walkers down the aisle. It is not unusual for your flight attendant to be well into her 70's with her eyes sporting more "air bags" than Ford Motor Company.

The number of times our sinus cavities have been pressurized and depressurized is only diminished by the radiation count flowing through our veins. Therefore, that healthy, youthful glow we possessed in our first year of flying is gone. We have developed calluses on our Achilles tendons from offending roll-a-bags and tally marks from meal flights in the form of burn scars trailing up our forearms.

Because our only on-the-job food source is salt-, carbohydrate-, and preservative-laced, and because we've probably borne children, some of us have gained weight in the past 20 years. Therefore, some of us are gradually becoming "C-D" girls (the seats we slam with our hips when waddling down the aisle—C, D, C, D, C, D, is how the cadence goes). Also, those flight attendants, who are younger than me, do not need to be reminded of their fading youth due to their fourth consecutive early morning wake-up call.

Even though you may only desire to start a conversation or show concern for our well-being, take note, our dilapidated physical appearance is not a wise thing to comment on.

I have been known to reply, "This is as good as it gets," because I had plenty of sleep the night before and for a change the bathroom mirror on that aircraft wasn't distorted like a fun house mirror to magnify every wrinkle in my dehydrated face. And I was feeling content with my appearance before that passenger astutely pointed out the "air bags" under my eyes. After that I moped in the galley for the duration of the flight.

The mystery of it all is—although your flight attendants have gotten *older*, your pilots are getting *younger*. Probably the reverse of your preference.

A few years ago, when one of my equally-aged coworkers introduced herself to the pilots in the cockpit at the start of her trip, she noticed the first officer's ID badge hanging from his jacket in the closet. A look of disbelief spread across her face as she proclaimed, "Hi, I'm Sheryl, and I used to change your diapers!"

Needless to say, the blushing pilot didn't request cockpit service from his former babysitter during that flight.

36

Tell a flight attendant to smile

Because passengers never say this to male flight attendants, their purpose in this statement must not be to cheer us up. Though I guess having a flight attendant mimic a Barbie doll for their personal pleasure might make *them* chuckle a bit.

One day I told a silly man who said this to me that he should smile for the duration of the flight, and I would come back to monitor his grin every five minutes.

Come on, give us a break. Flight attendants are never without an audience. We'd have to put Vaseline on our teeth to accomplish a 12-hour smile.

FYI—When you observe that vacant, hardened gaze in your FA's eyes and a slight frozen smirk upon her lips, she is not smiling at you. Your flight attendant is not with us anymore. She has escaped to her "happy place," the only defense against her breaking point of no return. It may be best to leave her alone for a while.

37

Pretend you have a personal servant

Foremost, remember this: Flight attendants are on the airplane for your safety. As often quoted, we are there to "*save* your 'butt,' not *kiss* it." But because you are our valued customers who ultimately pay our wages, we will try to make your trip comfortable—if you are reasonably polite.

If I have a coffeepot in one hand and enough trash in the other to top off a landfill, don't ask me to get the pillow in your overhead bin. (One, two—stretch those knees, inhale deeply . . . don't give up now . . . you can do it!) Ever hear of blood clots?

Don't throw your garbage on the floor and expect me to pick it up while your nose is buried in your newspaper. I don't do floors. Even the pilots can't get away with that. I think that will be my next book, *199 Ways in Which **Pilots** Make Flight Attendants Fly—Off the Handle!*

38

Pretend you don't speak English

Children hear what they want to hear, and some adults have also caught onto this ploy. I've found that, "We have a place in the closet for your bag," is much easier for some passengers to interpret than, "We'll need to check your bag."

39

Ring your call button often

There are some people who are hooked on that power-ful sensation of pushing a button with a picture of a slave on it...and having one suddenly appear. (Refer to Offense 37.) They usually just need their cup picked up, while I am expecting to administer first aid.

Pavlov's dog couldn't have been more conditioned to his buzzers than an FA is to the call chimes on an airplane. Even at home, we automatically glance at the ceiling when the doorbell rings. Not one flight attendant would miss a morning flight or hit that sleep button if our alarm clocks mimicked a passenger call bell.

Our training goes something like this: One ring means a passenger call or a seat belt sign has been turned on or off; two rings, crewmember call; three rings, communicate immediately with the cockpit; and so on. Don't mess with an FA's communication system unless you have an important concern. And *never* ring your call button while we are taxiing, landing, or in our climb unless you are prepared to have CPR performed on you—which we prefer to do on unconscious victims. When passengers ring their call button to have a cup picked up in severe turbulence, their primary intention must be to watch a flight attendant hit the ceiling of an airplane.

So, please, think of another way to entertain Junior than allowing him to play with the pretty, colorful buttons above his head.

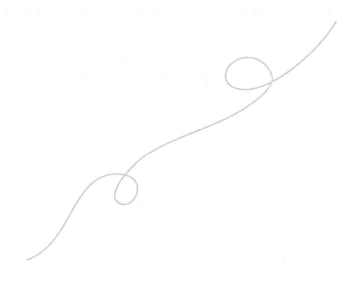

40

Pretend that the plane is a restaurant

Does it look like one? In reality, it is an *airplane*, and you're basically paying to get from Point A to Point B. Our added services and meals are just our pathetic attempt to make your journey more enjoyable. Look at anything beyond your transportation as an added bonus.

We don't have bottles of ketchup and mustard or packets of jelly and butter unless they come hermetically wrapped within your meal. We don't have a coat check, and we usually don't serve your salad first. And most important, we serve in the order that our carts are heading. We can't always come to your "table" for a leisurely chat.

There are certain instances where we are more than happy to wipe a spill, provide a sick-bag, obtain a Band-Aid, help a diabetic with his sugar intake or administer CPR—out of service-flow order. But if you are one of those "special" people who prefer their meal or drink before everyone else, please wait your turn.

41

Have all your body parts and possessions in the aisle

If you recall the tale about *The Princess and the Pea*, you will understand the sensitivity of our beverage carts to any foreign object in the aisle. Thin obstructions such as newspapers and magazines can easily send the hot coffee on my cart cascading to your lap.

If you are older than six, not incontinent, or not having digestive problems with our inflight delicacies, you should be able to time your bathroom trips. The carts we are pushing weigh well over 200 pounds, and our backs can't endure doing the cha-cha with a partner like that. Wait in your seat until the path is clear. Please don't tailgate on our heels while we're serving. We must dash to the galley frequently and may run over you before you know what hit you. This is also a reason to be mindful of your camouflaged purse strap protruding onto my raceway to the galley.

I was often grateful that my husband was not a jealous man, because I would often come home from work with new contusions encircling my upper thighs (the height of the passengers' elbows while typing on their laptops). Please, keep in mind that you may have bought an aisle seat, but not the aisle next to it.

I understand that your seat space has been diminished over the years, but it is still prudent to keep your feet, legs, elbows, and children out of the aisles for your and their own safety (remember that 200-pound cart).

42

Ignore us

Ignoring a flight attendant is common practice now that every passenger comes equipped with a laptop and head-phones as major accessories. And some passengers lead us to believe that we have their undivided attention, which merely turns out to be a pretense. It goes something like this:

"Would you like something to drink, sir?" I ask.

"What?" Oblivious passenger #57 looks toward me with headphones on his ears.

"Is your purse pink, sir?" I continue without fore-thought (because he's my 57th oblivious passenger).

"What?" He looks toward me with headphones still on ears.

"Do your shoes stink, sir?" Now I have the surrounding passengers, who are not accessorized with ear attach-ments, chuckling.

"What?" Still, he looks toward me with headphones on ears. At which point I feel the urge to peek under each earpiece to see if any gray matter has been sucked in.

At other times, passengers will totally disregard my presence. I will only ask twice before moving on to the next row (only my own husband and teenager could ignore me and get away with it). But inevitably, they will summon me back, while acting indignant and claiming they were skipped. Imagine this scenario 57 times.

Maybe passengers would duly take notice of my presence if I strolled through the aisle with garbage bag in hand, looked them in the eye and said, "*You're* trash?"

You're trash?

43

Use the first-class bins or bathrooms when you are seated in coach

Some passengers drag their luggage from their house to their car, through the parking lot to the airport, through security, to the gate, and down the jetway—but just can't find the energy to walk it past first-class and five feet farther to their seat in row 14. Because they are *banished* to coach, this must be their desperate attempt to upgrade a small token of their remaining ego to the luxuries of first class. This is also one of the 199 ways pilots choose to irritate us.

When coach bathrooms harbor long lines, it would be a shame not to use an empty first-class bathroom. And once again, if you're incontinent, under the age of six, or having problems digesting our airplane meals, you may not be able to wait until the carts clear a path to the coach bathroom. These are reasonable requests. But if you are not physically disabled and are merely too lazy to walk the extra 20 feet to the coach bathroom, just remember the possibility of those blood clots.

While we're on the subject of biffies, can anyone tell me why passengers pull on the square ashtray instead of turning the round doorknob to open the door? Ah, you recognized yourself, didn't you? To a flight attendant this is a most mysterious aviation phenomenon (besides the fact that we still have ash trays on airplane doors).

44

Roll your eyes if we don't have root beer

When it comes to eye-rolling, don't try to compete with a flight attendant—we've perfected it.

I pride myself on being able to list our beverage selectins in less than five seconds:

PepsiDietPepsi7Diet7gingeralemountaindewmineralwaterB ottledwaterorangeappletomatospiceytomatograpefruitcran berryJuicecoffeeteacocktailsbeerandwine...Phew! I'll bet you never get that many choices in a restaurant. (Refer to Offense 40)

Also keep in mind, when you are on an airplane always open sealed containers away from your Armani suit or Ann Taylor dress. Pressurization has an odd effect on potato chip bags, yogurt containers, and soda cans (being dropped in the galley doesn't help the latter).

If you complain about our soda selections, a less ethical flight attendant than me may be tempted to provide you that unopened soda can. And due to the lack of oven mitts on airplanes, flight attendants possess no fingerprints— there will never be physical evidence.

45

Contaminate our carts

Please do not help yourself to the items that are visibly displayed on our beverage carts. Throwing your garbage in the ice bucket, digging through the limes in the condiment cup, or licking your fingers to pinch a stir stick will not speed up service but will only spread your cold virus to the other 179 passengers.

Speaking of contamination, not only is there a "mile-high" club for lurid activities (see offense #81), but there seems to be a "mile-high" club for bodily functions as well. I swear that there are less airline tales on air rage than on random urinations. Or maybe they're connected, somehow.

Personally, I've witnessed a man who peed on the galley floor in front of me without blinking an eye. And some "pee"ple (sorry, couldn't help myself) have been more creative using other "portals" such as orange juice jugs, ice buckets, serving carts, and flight attendants' legs.

No, it is not a glamorous job (see offense # 77).

46

Do not place your tray table down when we reach your row

This would be fine if you plan to hold your coffee with one hand, open the three packets of sugar you requested with the second, and eat pretzels with the third. But if this isn't your intent, please put your tray table down so *I* don't have to grow a third hand to slap some sense into you.

47

Have your computer on the tray table when we're trying to place your meal there

Where would you like me to stick...I mean put your meal, Sir?

48

Have your newspaper blocking our reach to the window-seat passenger

I imagine that a Rorschach coffee-blot test on the commodity section would cure this irritating practice.

49

Wallow in pity if we forget your row

In most cases, a passenger has either been sleeping or sporting a noise-canceling headset when we, unsuccessfully, try to get their drink order. Although, sometimes we do make mistakes—because we are human (refer to Offense 83).

Don't take it personally—we are not purposely tormenting you. Instead of sticking out that lower lip and pouting, politely mention our oversight—you'll be served faster.

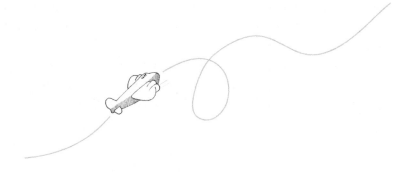

50

Hang around the galley

Please don't loiter in the galley unless you're George Clooney or exceptionally good-looking *and* over 18 years old. Our galley, on average, four feet wide. If we are in the middle of our service, to enter within is like strolling into the middle of a Spanish bull run.

If the galley curtain is closed, we are probably savoring our only meal of the day. Many times, we need to "dine" while standing over a garbage cart or sitting on an ice chest positioned in the middle of the galley floor. Don't peek your head in and hand us your dirty cup. Keep it on your tray, stick it in the seat pocket, or throw it at the man snoring behind you. We'll get to you eventually; we aren't leaving the premises.

If you insist on entering our meager workspace or intruding upon our cherished private time, you may experience a cart inadvertently wheeled over your foot or a perfected eye-roll.

51

Mumble when giving us your drink order

Besides the fact that your flight attendants are getting older, we have also been sandwiched between two droning engines with 40,000 pounds of thrust for approximately 23,000 hours of our lives. Needless to say, our hearing isn't what it used to be. Please raise your voice and face us when placing your order so we can lip-read.

I highly respect any foreign passenger who speaks or attempts (Offense 38) to speak English. And for those whom I ask to repeat, please bear with me as I try to decipher. Also, an apology is in order for those passengers in the past when I was not yet culturally suave.

Before four mergers and two buyouts (I've been bought and sold more than a knick-knack at a garage sale), I was employed with a relatively small airline. The most glamorous, exotic route available was on a 727 from Minneapolis to Denver. Needless to say, my exposure to other cultures was limited to the Amish of Pennsylvania or the rednecks south of the Mason Dixon Line.

So back in those ignorant days on a flight from Minneapolis to Kansas City, I encountered a well-dressed Japanese businessman seated at the window seat of a DC-9. After asking if he would like a beverage, he nodded his head, waved his hand back and forth, and said "Tanka." Anxious to oblige, I ran to the galley and mixed our only hot, decaffeinated beverage available.

I now understand his look of confusion when presenting him with a cup of Sanka for both beverage services, and the reason the two full cups were still sitting on his tray for landing.

As the polite Japanese populace do, he was only nodding in appreciation, waving his hand "no" and saying "Thank you" with a Japanese accent.

52

Ask for an extra meal

To be truthful, this request will surprise more than irritate us.

This used to be a more common occurrence when Hulk Hogan and his comrades from the WCW flew my airline. Now that meal *services* are infrequent, and meal *shortages* are frequent and frustrating occurrences for flight attendants, to ask this is usually futile.

Furthermore, if you are flying domestically in main cabin (we try not to refer to this cattle car as "second class"), bring your plastic and count on paying for any morsel of nutrition.

53

Order a special meal and don't claim it

If you haven't changed your religion, medical history, or fad diet since you've booked your flight, please claim that special meal when we come to your row. The airline does not put on extra smoked turkey sandwiches in case you've miraculously been cured of diabetes.

Furthermore, there is really nothing "special" about a special meal, except that it e-special-ly slows down the flow of our meal service. I once had 3 kosher, 4 child, 2 diabetic, 1 low-carb, 3 low-salt, and 10 vegetarian meals all ordered on one flight booked with only 98 passengers.

Now *that's* special.

54

See how many times you can make us run to the galley

When you request tea, an extra meal, or a soda during our galley break (Offense 50), for each of which we need to make a special trip, please ask for all your desires at once.

When new acquaintances inquire about my occupation, I like to tell them that I walk to California and back every day. Although this is not exactly my job description, I do spend most of time on my feet. Please don't add extra wear and tear to my bunions by asking for a tea for your spouse *after* I've returned from the galley with yours.

But, if your intent is to experience that perfected flight attendant eye-roll, this is one way to achieve it.

55

Get upset when you don't get a meal choice

Come on, now, you've had our meals—chicken or beef, what's the difference? There are so many preservatives used that most of us call it "mystery meat" anyway. When I run out of choices, some passengers act as if I've just informed them that they have only one month to live.

One day after an elderly lady in the last row disbelievingly exclaimed, "There's *no* choice?" I responded kindly, but firmly, "Yes, there is. To eat or not to eat." She looked at me slyly, shook her finger and teased, "You must be a mom!"

Yes, ma'am, in more than one way.

56

Complain about the meals

Wouldn't you think with all the griping about our food, that every passenger would be thrilled if we ran out?

One day on a flight to San Diego, there was a woman seated in coach cabin who believed she was destined to be in first-class. (Refer to Offense 22.) We call this type of passenger a "First-Class Wannabe." She spent most the flight crossing that formidable "Great Wall of Curtain" between the two sections. She requested the first-class champagne and ice cream dessert and refused to lower herself to use the coach bathroom. (Refer to Offenses 26 and 43.) Then, after hanging out in the first-class galley for most the flight (Offense 50), she felt the need to inform me how horrible the main-cabin meal was. So, acting surprised to the best of my ability, I told her that I personally thought the sandwich was savory. She looked down her nose and told me that I must not eat in the finest restaurants (Offense 40).

On another flight, a fellow flight attendant reached his limit when a passenger complained about a bad potato in her casserole dish. At some point in our careers, we all get to that breaking point after experiencing a few hundred wannabes, teenagers with headsets, business people with newspapers, and screaming flight-orphaned children. The FA in question abruptly grabbed the passenger's knife from her tray and threateningly waved it in the air. Then he proceeded to gingerly tap the potato on her tray in a chastising manner. He scolded, "BAD, potato! BAD, potato!"

When done, he gently set the knife back down and calmly informed her that the spud wouldn't bother her again.

Usually, if your potato is "bad," the chicken is still frozen, or your dish has tiny bugs making a home in the peas, we want to know—after all, we eat the meals ourselves. But if you are a finicky eater or merely accustomed to eating at the "finest restaurants," it's best to keep that to yourself.

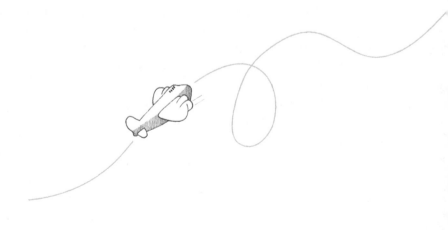

57

Parents, don't discuss with Junior his beverage choice before the cart gets to your row

Some parents know their beverage choice on the spot but have no clue what their toddler wants. When finally realizing this, they then ask their three-year old—which leaves me biding my time while watching the equivalent of a show host interviewing a bad guest. After a few minutes have passed, I proceed to ask Junior myself, and inevitably, he will look at me with a blank gaze and order root beer.

58

Parents, don't be aware that your kid will kick the seatback in front of them

To avoid the wrath of Mr. stressed-out businessman who will inevitably be seated there, be forewarned. However, you may not want to waste this opportunity; it could make for a great parenting moment (Refer to Offense 62).

With that in mind and when traveling with young children, it may be tempting to keep those separated seats that were assigned to you. Although I have found that most families, to their credit, want to sit together. And even though your flight attendants prefer that your children sit with you, we can't force passengers to change seats. Your luck will depend on the kindness of your fellow passengers, and I wouldn't chance it.

Checking in online within 24-hours or being early at the airport might help (Refer to Offense 1). But sadly, the world is motivated by financial gain. So, if you and your children didn't get seat assignments together, it could be that you bought "economy" tickets. Because I sympathize with the daunting monetary burden it must be to buy tickets for an entire family, I'll let you in on an old secret of mine.

Approach your child, who will inevitably be seated in a middle seat on a full airplane, and exclaim (audibly for adjacent seat mates), "Here's a bag, honey, I'm seated two rows back. Let me know when you need to throw up again."

There are usually no guarantees in life, but this has worked for me every time.

59

Parents, be helpless

Flight attendants find it quite odd that a single parent with four kids can conduct his or her journey more efficiently than can two parents and grandma with only one child.

Even though we are usually happy to be of aid to parents in need when they are overwhelmed with air travel, please don't ask me to clean the puke off your child's lap. If you don't bring the essentials for your children, or expect us to carry and stow your bags, or babysit your kids, either you didn't plan well for the trip or you adopted your children yesterday.

60

Believe that toddlers can safely bounce off ceilings

I could possibly understand the foolishness of letting your kid run through the aisle in times of severe weather turbulence if you were taking the same risk. But I've always wanted to ask, why do you bother fastening your seat belt when your child is using the seat next to you as a trampoline?

61

Hand us a dirty diaper

Flight attendants have been exposed to so many germs that I believe we would be the last surviving species after a biological warfare. Nevertheless, there's something about that damp, warm bundle of body waste that will send a chill up any FA's spine when it is placed in her hand and her fingers inadvertently wrap around it.

Your kid is cute; his diaper is not. Place it in a sick-bag and throw it in the bathroom trash where it belongs. You can hand us your germ-laden glass or a regurgitated sandwich on a plate, but *do not* hand us Junior's dirty diaper. (Do you want your meal served with that same hand?)

62

Parents, don't be the adult

Most flight attendants like children—quiet, polite children that is. Many of us have munchkins of our own, so we understand that even the most well-behaved child will deviate at times. And babies cry—there's no getting around that. But please remember, your parenting skills do not stop at the airplane door.

Calling all parental troops! You must take control before miniature aliens take over our plane(t)!

If you cannot control Junior, we can't either. I wish I had a foot massage for every time a parent calmly proclaims, "But he won't stay seated." Are they confessing to a parental defect? I can almost envision a white flag of surrender waving above their heads.

63

Passengers without kids,
don't be an adult

Please don't involve us, we must referee our own kids at home.

If somebody's seatback is in your meal tray, graciously ask him or her to move it up—it works every time. If someone's kid is kicking your seatback, politely ask the child to stop—it works every other time.

64

Walk barefoot, or let your child walk barefoot, on an airplane

This will make the most composed flight attendant cringe. Even if that carpet is cleaned every week (which it isn't), I guarantee that within a single day someone will have either puked or broken a glass there.

65

Forget your manners

What ever happened to the words "please" and "thank you"? And this is coming from a person who thanks you for handing her your trash.

When I am taken for granted, it always gives me a déjà vu of my childrearing days. If, while boarding, you hit me in the head with your backpack, run over my Achilles with your roll-a-bag or body check me onto the lap of the nearest aisle passenger, a simple "sorry" will do. Flight attendants have feelings too.

66

Don't listen to the announcements

There is something inexplicable about this particular announcement, "The captain has just turned on the fasten-seat-belt sign. Please remain seated with your seat belts securely fastened," which makes every passenger feel the urge to use the bathroom. And on most flights, there will undoubtedly be two passengers trying to yell their conversation over the safety announcement as I give the preflight demonstration in front of them. I have often contemplated the length of that oxygen mask cord while demonstrating its use.

As irrelevant as it may seem, we sometimes announce where the reading light button is located, yet this is a frequent inquiry from our passengers after the fact. There is one flight attendant who dryly informs his passengers that their reading light works like a "clapper" switch. I've seen him double over with laughter behind the galley curtain while observing the willing participant determinedly applaud the light bulb above his or her head.

I know that the prerequisite for doctors is terrible handwriting and for pilots mumbled speech, but your flight attendants usually speak clearly in English when it is our first language. If you are not attentive, you never know when you might miss something more important than the flight time.

For example: "Ladies and gentlemen, if you look off to your right, you may catch a glimpse of Mt. St. Helens erupting," or "Ladies and gentlemen, we may run out of meals on our flight today, but if you choose to have the fish casserole left over from yesterday's flight, we'll give you a free package of Imodium tablets," or "Ladies and gentlemen, welcome on board flight 325. We will notify you of our destination as soon as this information is obtained from the man in the cockpit with an Uzi". (Refer to Offense 68.)

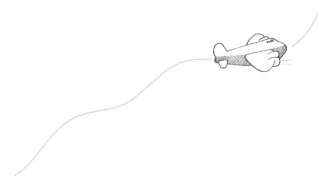

67

Joke about carrying a bomb or weapon

The University of Minnesota hockey team had to perform without a player in the 1974 national championships in Boston because their jokester goalie didn't heed this airline "no-no" while going through airport security. Can you say *detainment*?

68

Try to take over the aircraft

I'm sure the vast majority of you readers have never had that thought cross your mind. And I don't believe it would do any good to remind the small minority who have, that the end results are either:

    1. You will spend your life behind bars.

         or

    2. You will die.

After the events that occurred on 9-11, your crew-members are no longer alone in their efforts to maintain control of the ship. We now have the vast majority behind us.

69

Use the word "crash" in your speech

After entering through the steel portals of the aircraft door, remember this—you "impacted" the car last week, you "suddenly fell asleep" last night, and the stock market "took a dive" yesterday.

70

Call your flight attendant a "stewardess"

If you aren't yet aware—we haven't been called that for at least 50 years. I'm sure this change of title happened around the same time "garbage men" became "sanitation workers" and "swamps" became "wet-lands."

You may have heard flight attendants use the term "stewardess" or "stew" within their own ranks. The privilege for this term's usage lies solely there, because in this environment it is used only in jest.

If you are an outsider to the ranks, it shows ignorance to call us "stewardesses." We've even stopped getting upset over it—we'll just look at you with pity.

71

Take it out on us when the airline loses your bag or charges too much for your ticket

As a frontline employee I realize that I represent my company—but I am not its whipping boy.

If you have a legitimate complaint and diplomatically make me aware of it, you will receive every perk within my reach to show apology from the airline. Remember though, my powers of contrition are limited to a free headset, drink, or mileage coupon—not my firstborn.

72

Believe that you'll receive a free ticket or a first-class seat if you complain enough

Please don't gripe about the disappearance of peanuts from our snack list. Most airlines have ceased peddling peanuts because some passengers are deathly allergic to the little tidbit. Foremost, it's never wise to complain to flight attendants about over-efficient security even if you've been strip-searched there. We go through the same scrutiny. Besides the source of your inconvenience may have saved our lives a thousand times over. And during the anthrax scare after 9-11, the passengers, who became upset by the absence of dry creamers on the airplanes, must have lived in some remote cave without media.

Don't get me wrong, there are many legitimate complaints about air travel. Yet, if you are merely searching for a problem with the sole purpose of receiving something for free, an FA can spot you a mile away (e.g., The attorney who handed me his card and claimed I had fractured his foot, which had been extended into the middle of the aisle before I inadvertently "tapped" it with an empty meal cart).

On an airplane, the squeaky wheel does not get the grease but merely the "greasiest" chicken casserole.

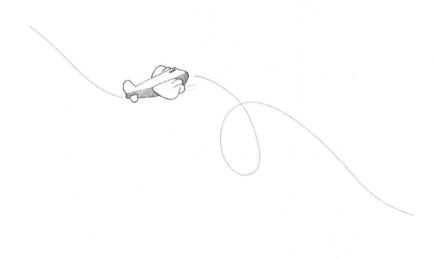

73

Call your flight attendant names

Believe me, you do not want to be the straw that broke the stew's (term allowed here) back. Name-calling does not happen often, and to give my passengers some credit, it hasn't happened to me in 40 years. Even so, I cannot help but share this story with you.

Years ago, at about 30,000 feet above the earth, a passenger got snippy with an FA (imagine that); then the FA got snippy back (imagine that). And so on and so forth it went. When the tension peaked, it was the passenger who reached his breaking point first.

He exclaimed to his winged adversary, "You're a witch!" Without a moment's hesitation, the flight attendant in question waved her finger in the air like a wand, pointed it at the offender and retorted, "Poof! Then you're a pile of sh**!"

Although I do not condone this flight attendant's response, one has to admire her quick wit. Besides, she turned him back before landing.

74

Verbally abuse your flight attendant

If you need to relay the saga of that two-hour wait at the ticket counter with the intention that the word will reach management, speak calmly, without yelling, and you will be better understood. Better yet, write to the management. I have the address and you have a lot more pull than I do.

As soon as you yell or curse at me (FAR 121.580), I will tune you out and your words will not reach their destination. And, most likely, neither will you.

75

Physically abuse your flight attendant

There once was a time when a flight attendant could immediately tell when a passenger was a little "off". Now that Bluetooth ear buds are commonly used, *everyone* seems to be talking to themselves.

As a result, your flight attendants can't always identify these "off" people before we push back from the gate and "air rage" has become a popular term in the airline industry. I've only had one minor instance that comes close, and I didn't see it coming.

As we were taxiing down the runway in preparation for take-off, I noticed a woman standing in the aisle (Offense 3, again). After my repeated attempts to politely inform her that she must take her seat (Offense 23), she covered her ears with her hands and proceeded to "sing" over my voice.

Okay, maybe her carpet didn't go wall-to-wall, but at that moment I reached that infrequent but inevitable FA "breaking point." I informed her that I had ample experience dealing with the likes of her because of my 4-year-old at home. I admit that my comment deserved some kind of retort, but I did not anticipate a vigorous kick to my forearm.

Some airlines have a special tool at hand for situations

like this. It is an official, laminated note called "Notification of Violation" that describes the penalty for accosting your flight attendant: an immediate return to the airport for the accoster's arrest.

Coincidently, after I handed her that card, the captain's voice came over the PA announcing that we were experiencing a problem that needed some attention and were returning to the gate. The woman in question never realized, nor did I enlighten her, that we had returned to the gate for a malfunctioning wing flap and not because of her deviant behavior. Consequently, she straightened up for the rest of the flight.

If you are ever presented with this long-winded, official, four-page laminated document, I will save you the time of deciphering the legal jargon. It simply translates, "Proceed directly to jail. Do not pass Go."

76

Make lewd comments to your flight attendant

When a 19-year-old passenger told me that "older women make beautiful lovers," maybe I would have been flattered had he not been visually impaired from alcohol consumption. And I probably deserved the proposition by that 70-year-old Slavic man, after I repeated the words that my Slovenian grandma use to yell at the 32 grandchildren who invaded her home every Thanksgiving. Lesson I learned—know the language before you speak it.

Yet, with these exceptions, always remember that crude comments are usually offensive to your flight attendant. Aside from the fact that a bawdy proposition could be considered an infringement of the law called *sexual harassment*, gone are the days of the "stewardess" (refer to Offense 70). The old slogan "Marry me and fly free!" is now more aptly stated, "Propose? And why? To fly standby?"

Some of us are now appropriately called "Slam-Clickers," which mimics the sound of the hotel room door shutting and locking until wake-up the next morning. We no longer choose overnights to acquaint ourselves with pilots over dinner, but to acquire per diem pay while savoring canned tuna in front of the TV in our hotel rooms.

You'll find that most flight attendants do not apply for the job to *find* a family, but to *support* one. And we are probably not staring at you because we think you're cute but are merely mesmerized by the penne pasta hanging from your moustache.

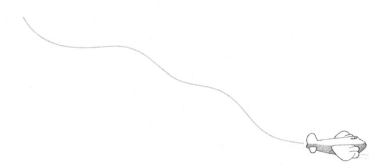

77

Believe that being a flight attendant is glamorous

Yes, we do travel to some exotic places, which become less exotic with each trip. By the 57th time we see Hong Kong, we have reverted to our slam-click ways. By the third trip to Grand Forks, North Dakota, we are qualified to be tour guides there, and by the second visit to New York's JFK Airport, we wish we had listened to our fathers before applying for our airline jobs.

Even though we are professionals in our field and highly trained in first aid and emergency procedures, face it, what we normally do is serve stale sandwiches, troubleshoot passenger complaints and pick up trash for a living—if all goes as planned. Believe me, I have searched through every slimy overhead bin, greasy garment closet, and rancid trash cart—and I have yet to find the glamour in my job.

78

Have your priorities in the wrong order

I once had a gentleman on my flight who was upset about not being served in a timely manner. Though, I believe he must have noticed the flight attendants assisting the nurse who was administering an IV for the passenger across the aisle.

Another time, a passenger complained to me that he had missed a connection because the flight attendants on his last flight insisted that an unconscious passenger, on a stretcher, deplane before him.

I refrained from presenting him my perfected eye-roll and responded with silence—but I really wanted to tell him that I would be happy to push him off in a stretcher as well.

79

Ask us to call ahead to hold your connecting flight

In this new, "fast-track" era, most airlines do not delay a flight for connecting passengers. If this were their policy, your next flight would be delayed and the next after that, and so on. Imagine the domino effect that would have throughout the country.

On the brighter side, with this new age of technology, we don't have to notify anyone of your delayed flight or your location, because all that information is in the airline's computer system. It may give you a warm, cozy feeling to know that your connecting gate agent knows exactly where you are when he sends the airplane off without you.

80

Assume all male flight attendants are gay

They aren't. To leave no doubt, the straight male flight attendants are easily recognized by one or more of the following:

1. He exhibits an exaggerated macho walk (e.g., not allowing the upper arms to touch the ribcage).

2. The female FA on the jumpseat next to him has only one "cheek" to sit on because his legs are spread as far apart as possible.

3. If single, he will perceptibly flirt with the women passengers.

4. If married, he will have pictures of his wife, children, or hunting dog visibly displayed.

81

Venture to join the mile-high club

For those who aren't familiar with the term, this activity is usually attempted in our 3×3 ×7-square-foot bathrooms in a vertical position and *usually* requires two people in attendance (not necessarily of the opposite sex). If you must join this club, please try to be quiet and quick so as not to inconvenience our less playful passengers.

Because your flight attendants are trained to be observant on the job, you are likely to be "exposed," so to speak. Don't be surprised as you exit the biffy in the aftermath to find an applauding audience, and your flight attendants displaying one-through-ten score cards. It's been done.

In addition to being quiet and quick, we prefer that your initiation take place *in the confines* of the bathrooms. A lesson was learned by two first-class passengers in seats 1A and 1B (mostly in 1A) on one of my flights to Las Vegas.

Though it was a "redeye" flight and the cabin lights were low, by mid-flight I was getting pretty tired of the continuous, guttural whispers originating from around the corner from the galley. As I debated whether to empty my water pitcher in the drain or somewhere else, I received an important message from the cockpit.

The captain informed me that we had an escaped bank robber on our aircraft and gave me a physical description of him. During the flight, we were to visually and discretely scope out the passengers who most resembled that profile. Then at our destination we were to alert the police, stationed in the jetway, with a nod as the suspects exited the airplane.

I was pretty sure the passenger in 12D fit the description they gave me. And even though the guy under the girl under the blanket in 1A neither had dark hair nor was over six feet tall—hey, it could have been him!

Upon our arrival and after nodding to the officers in the jetway at the Las Vegas airport, the wrinkled, flushed couple's bags were searched as they left my flight. Well, the marked bills were found on Mr. 12D after all, but I was filled with civic pride after authorities confiscated 20 grams of cocaine from my frisky first-class passengers!

Remember, PDAs (public displays of affection) make our passengers uncomfortable and irritate your flight attendant, who may not have seen her husband for a while.

82

Pretend that you aren't in the old U.S. of A.

Though we are very respectful of other cultures, when it comes down to a passenger committing Offense 26 or Offense 37, flight attendants draw the line. American women are progeny of the Suffragettes and have been genetically influenced by "burn the bra" slogans and the women's rights campaign.

If you are from a country that doesn't recognize women as equals and are flying within the US—check the attitude with your bag at the ticket counter before you board an American carrier. After all, when *I'm* in Rome, I do what the Romans do.

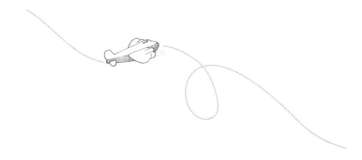

83

Believe that flight attendants have superpowers

We flight attendants are quite a confused breed. One minute, a passenger may treat us as though we're blubbering airheads and then, in next breath, expect the impossible from us.

Note: We do not have a photographic memory. Thus, we cannot, on demand, recite the gate information for 170 connecting passengers. Besides, we hesitate to give this information because it becomes obsolete once we land.

Note: Most of us (although I've heard we have one witch, refer to Offense 73) do not have the psychic ability to know which state, lake, or mountain range we are flying over. We normally don't gaze out the window while attempting to serve 170 meals.

Note: I know for a fact, that there is not one flight attendant in our hire who possesses X-ray eyes to see if your bag made it into the belly of our aircraft.

84

Use sign language when needing attention

Some passengers may have grown up a middle child, as I did—but I got over it. Here is a new language developed by a few of our first-class passengers.

Shaking the ice in your glass.

Interpretation: I want another drink.

Holding your glass in the air.

Interpretation: I want you to take my trash.

Standing in the aisle with your jacket dangling from one finger while blankly staring at your flight attendant.

Interpretation: I want you to hang my coat.

Even my toddlers' efforts at communication were more creative.

85

Claim that your poodle is a service animal

Service animals are wonderful creatures bringing much utility and comfort to their owners. Please don't muddy their reputation just so you can hold Fifi on your lap during the flight. And if you bribed your chiropractor (who happens to be your brother-in-law) to write a note claiming that your pet will help calm your anxiety, and then the animal behaves worse than a child—I'm not buying it.

I have observed that airlines are not discriminatory toward genuine service animals. The pet can legitimately be of any race excluding reptile, rodent, or arachnid. Keeping this in mind, if your pet is a service animal of any ethnicity, it should be on your lap or on the floor—it should not be sitting on a passenger seat (that right is exclusively reserved for Bullseye, the Target dog).

Porky the pig may be cute, but its back end, most likely, does not smell pretty. It's true, we have seen it all.

86

Take your pet out of its carrier during the flight

I like most animals—I have a couple of my own. But one of my biggest "pet" peeves is when Fluffy's owner insists on removing her from the carrier beneath the seat because she is meowing—the owner being completely oblivious to the 10 percent of the passengers who are allergic to cats. Not to confuse the plane with a restaurant (Offense 40), but we also may be serving food nearby. Fluffy will be just fine if you merely give her a mild sedative before the flight. As a matter of fact, she will then be my happiest passenger.

If you plan on flying your pet to Aunt Betsy's house over Christmas, you must inform the airline when you make your reservation, pay an additional fee, and provide signed documentation of vaccination history at check-in. Even if you are able get your pet past security and the gate agent without doing so, there are still your attentive flight attendants to deal with.

Finally (I've been wanting to say this since Paris Hilton started a new trend): **A dog is an animal.** Please, keep it in its carrier until you're away from a public place *and* you're assured that everyone in its vicinity likes animals. Your pet doesn't need to walk through the airport until it relieves itself on the nearest kiosk, and it doesn't need a baby stroller.

I'm not kidding, this is what it's come to. It's evident that priorities are at an all-time low when children are on leashes and dogs are in buggies.

87

Smoke in the bathrooms or anywhere near the airplane

If you're hooked on nicotine, as I once was, check your cigarettes with your luggage and expect to go through many hours of withdrawal if you're booked on a flight that day. Refer to Offense 3, Offense 23, Offense 66 and, last but not least, refer, in the Glossary, to the fatal Air Canada flight 797.

88

If you're a doctor, nurse, or EMT, don't respond to a medical emergency

Your flight attendants are trained only in the basics of first aid and life support. Please, we need your help!

On one of my flights, after I paged for a doctor to no avail, I found myself doing CPR on a gentleman who was lying in the aisle. A passenger in the aisle seat was acting as a "backseat driver" by critiquing my work. He wasn't much help but merely an annoyance. Had I known at that time that he was a doctor, who did not want to get involved, I would have been more than annoyed.

Since the Aviation Medical Assistance Act went into effect and there are "good Samaritan" laws in every state, I find numerous professionals volunteering in any emergency situation. Thank you, thank you, thank you. As a matter of fact, I would bet my metal wings that more doctors will respond to an emergency and their response time will be quicker on an airplane than in a hospital emergency room.

A special thank-you goes to one of my volunteers, who was *both* an EMT *and* fluent in Russian. He came in quite handy when an elderly Russian passenger had a heart attack. Because we were flying from Minneapolis to Grand Forks, I consider that the epitome of a coincidence.

89

Beat your neighbor to the aisle before the airplane arrives at the gate

Some passengers, noncompliant with the FARs and at the risk of being rude, like to stand up before the seat belt sign is turned off in order to get ahead of a few fellow passengers.

This way they, cleverly, achieve a 6.2-minute wait instead of 6.5-minute wait to exit from the rear of a 757. Or, best-case scenario, they exit the airplane a whole three minutes sooner and wait at baggage claim a whole three minutes longer.

90

Be the first one out of your seat if you move slower than a snail

Wheelchairs don't normally arrive at the airplane until every passenger has deplaned. So, if you need some wheels, there is no need to hold up the other passengers by butting in front of them.

Whether you're elderly, high, or merely possess a mellow personality, please don't shuffle in front of those "A" types. Trust me, *they* will not slow you down.

91

Strive to be the last one off the airplane

About 99 percent of our passengers want to be the first one off the airplane (their chances are, at best, one in 170). But believing the odds are much better, there is one person who strives to be the *last* one off. The cleaners cannot clean, the caterers cannot cater, and the gate agents cannot re-board the airplane if you wait until every person is off before rising from your seat in a leisurely manner.

Hurry up; slow down. I know this is getting a little confusing. But if you think of the term "cattle drive" and move evenly with the crowd, you'll be just fine.

92

Believe that a "direct" flight will not stop in Denver or Atlanta

You'll find that the term "direct" is a more liberal one than "nonstop" when it comes to describing flights. Refer to the Glossary.

93

Stay on the airplane when on a "through" flight

So, you opted to book your direct flight in order to not change planes, and the flight attendants ask you to deplane?

They will explain that you may prefer to stay out of the cleaners' way, stretch your legs (in re, those blood clots), or check out the salsas in the Phoenix airport gift shop. And they'll also convince you that those options are more rewarding than breathing the circulated, jet-fuel-saturated air on the plane.

What they won't mention is that the crew bus may run every thirty minutes, and your flight attendants can't get off the aircraft until *you* leave.

94

Leave a mess

Even though flight attendants don't normally clean airplanes, we are thoroughly disgusted with the condition in which some passengers leave their seat areas.

Even if your spouse cleans up after you at home, I know you can refrain from scattering 57 pages of newspaper across the aisle. And though you're a working parent and have a full-time housekeeper, I have confidence that you can direct your kids, just this once, to throw their Cheerios in my trash bag instead of on the floor.

95

Take someone else's wheelchair

Apart from taking candy from a baby, this is the lowest. If you didn't request a wheelchair with your reservation, you may have to wait until the more forward thinkers claim theirs first.

96

Order a wheelchair and then don't claim it

We call these incidents "inflight miracles." We don't really understand what heals our previously disabled passengers, allowing them to walk off the airplane unassisted (we know it's not the food).

Let your flight attendant know if you don't want that wheelchair you ordered. Because all the wheel-chairs in the airport may be waiting at planes for nonexistent riders, the elderly woman at the next plane who was *not* cured during the flight must wait longer for hers.

97

Take 57 snapshots of Junior in the cockpit when we're done deplaning

Pilots and flight attendants alike enjoy educating and entertaining our young passengers with a trip to the cockpit. However, please, ask at the beginning of the flight when that visit would be most appropriate.

If you wait till deplaning, please, don't loiter too long or wait for your child to conclude the visit. The captain's last flight home may soon depart, and the next crew bus will barely give me time to make *my* son's football game.

98

Ask a flight attendant, in the gate area, for directions as you deplane

Have you ever noticed a mysterious-looking person in a flight attendant uniform, minus the wings and name tag, wearing dark sunglasses and conveniently seated behind that obese man in the corner of the gate area? Exactly my point.

We can get very creative when trying to be *incognito* off the airplane. Flight attendants get paid only when all three of the following are true: (1) We are on the aircraft, (2) the door is closed, and, (3) the brakes are released. Don't interrupt our unpaid break, please.

Gate agents, on the other hand, are on the time clock until they punch out at the end of their shift. Also, they work in that airport every day and can more suitably answer your questions. That flight attendant sitting in the gate area devouring the Chicago hot dog has no idea where baggage claim is in O'Hare because she has spent her 30 minutes between flights waiting in a concession line.

Gate agents and flight attendants may all look alike, both possessing similar uniforms and hardened, vacant stares, but *gate* agents are usually the ones standing behind the *gate* (key word here) podium with a mile-long passenger line in front of them.

Better yet, don't bother them either; there are gigantic signs and TV monitors throughout every airport to explicitly point you to any destination.

99

Take yourself too seriously

Finding humor in your own idiosyncrasies is not only a rare talent but also a very useful one; you can easily entertain yourself wherever you go.

And I know that if I continue to find humor in my job, I will possibly make it through the next 6 years to retirement.

You must admit that humans are funny animals. After all, if we can't laugh at ourselves, someone else will!

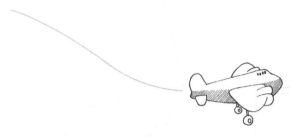

Cleared for landing...

Now that we are on our final descent, I realize that the information revealed here could be used to a flight attendant's disadvantage. Yet, I know that my astute readers would never be that ignorant after having been educated on the finer points of air travel. That would be crazier than calling me "stewardess."

I ask that you merely remember some of the old adages that your parents may have recited:

- Don't bite the hand that feeds you.
- Don't look a gift horse in the mouth.
- Be polite to "the help"; you don't know what goes on in the kitchen.
- Pick on someone your own size.

Which all leads back to my initial purpose for this book: A better understanding of how **not** to make your next flight attendant fly off the handle. Besides, we "stews" are merely ninety-nine ways away from a beer and a slide into early retirement!

Landing.

Ladies and gentlemen, we have reached our final destination. Please remain seated until we have come to a complete stop at the last page. The local *time* now is *to take action.* If you need to make a *connection* between your viewpoint and mine, the flight attendant on your next flight will be happy to assist you. As you deplane, please recommend this reading material to your fellow travelers.

On behalf of myself and my publishing crew members, thank you for flying with us. We hope you consider us the next time your intellect requires literary travel.

Bah-bye now!

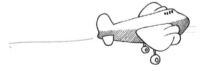

Glossary

ABP—Able-bodied person. A passenger sitting at an emergency exit who agrees to assist the FA at that exit in case of an evacuation. *A passenger whose true intent is to achieve extra legroom.

AC—Aircraft or airplane. *A circular tube flying approximately 30,000 feet above the ground (aka an FA's office).

Air Canada Flight 797—Aviation accident on June 2, 1983, which killed 23 people, possibly due to disposal of a cigarette in the lavatory trash. *One dramatic example of a passenger ignoring one of the "silly" rules FAs try to enforce.

backscatter security scanner—Advanced imaging technology often referred to as a full-body scanner or the "naked machine." *A passenger's apprehension and a TSA's bane.

base—The city an FA works out of. *Often a city the FA doesn't actually live in.

boarding—Process in which passengers are allowed to enter the airplane. *The reason gate agents and FAs have a high rate of ulcers.

bulkhead seat—Any airplane seat behind a wall. *The most misunderstood seat on the airplane.

captain—Pilot in charge of the airplane and its operation. *The pilot who gets the most pay for doing something really important though nobody knows what that is.

cockpit—The locked area the pilots occupy to fly the airplane. *Now preferred to be called a "flight deck" (yet such an appropriate name is hard to drop).

connection—A change of aircraft at intermediate cities. *The difference between your arrival flight's gate number and your connecting flight's gate number usually diminishes the combined ages of your flight attendants.

crew bus—Provided by the airline to transport employees to and from the employee parking lots. *Unlike an FA, is not required to maintain a reliable schedule and takes longer to get to its destination than most flights.

deplaning—Process in which passengers are allowed to exit the airplane. *Much faster than boarding. Can sometimes be premature.

deregulation—An act of the government to have all airlines enter into the free marketplace of American business. *An act of government creating airlines with weird names that last only long enough to temporarily lower the profits of larger airlines.

direct flight—A flight that may stop at one or more intermediate cities between your departure city and your arrival city. Maintains the same flight number and aircraft. *Definition not written in stone, yet not to be confused with a "nonstop" flight.

E-Machine—Convenient electronic device that allows you to check in for your flight before proceeding to the gate of departure. *Getting an E-ticket from an E-Machine can E-zily help avoid waiting in line.

EMT—Emergency Medical Technician. Usually stationed on ambulances. *FAs would like one stationed on every flight.

FA—Flight attendant. Never referred to as "stewardess." *The only employee on aircraft who doesn't sit down on the job.

first officer—Second pilot in charge. *In absence of the second officer, pilot who does most the work but gets the least pay.

galley—Area in an aircraft for stowage of service items. *The 10 × 3-foot area in an aircraft "designed" (used loosely) to accommodate 100-plus meals (aka, an FA's kitchen).

gate—The numbered area in the airport from which you must board and deplane an aircraft. *The numbered area for your departing flight that is farthest away from the numbered area of your arriving flight.

gate-check—A process of checking your bag at the gate of departure. *Rarely voluntary.

garment closet—Closet on an airplane. Designed to hang passengers' garment bags. *Garment closets are for garment bags—not computer bags, roll-a-bags, or the framed velveteen image of Elvis Presley you bought in Mexico.

Good Samaritan Law—A law that has been enacted in every state. It protects medical personnel and citizens from lawsuits resulting from a sincere attempt to save someone's life. *A law that has benefited more FAs than the politicians will ever know.

inflight shoes—A pair of shoes an FA changes into once on the airplane. *The most comfortable, most hideous-looking shoes an FA can buy, that break the maximum number of airline dress-code rules.

jetway—The ramp that connects the airplane to the airport. *A 120° tunnel in New Orleans; a -30°F tunnel in Fargo.

jumpseat—A fold-out seat attached to the wall of the airplane, exclusively for flight attendant use. *Designed by airlines to discourage sitting.

lead flight attendant—FA who is responsible for the safety of the passengers, crew, and the service of her flight. Position is bid in seniority order. *FA frequently called at home after a trip for any deviation of circumstances beyond her control and is usually paid $2 more an hour for this responsibility. Position usually bid to the most junior FA.

nonstop flight—A flight that goes from departure city to arrival city without stopping. *Not written in stone.

O-dark-thirty check-in—An early morning departure. *Another reason why you shouldn't ask an FA to smile.

overnight—Any trip that includes an overnight stay in a hotel. *A trip that allows an FA a warm bath and her husband an education in fatherhood.

per diem—In addition to the basic wages, a dollar amount per hour paid to an FA for time away from her base. *An hourly stipend far below minimum wage, not worthy of missing your kid's baseball game.

predeparture drink—Beverage served to first-class passengers during boarding. *A singular term.

PSA or CSA—Passenger or customer service agent (aka gate agent). Uniformed airline employee who checks the passengers in for their flight and does various other jobs pertaining to such service. *The only other airline employee who receives as much abuse as an FA.

ramp rats—Another name for the ground personnel who load baggage, direct planes into gates, and perform various other jobs pertaining to such service. *Should be regarded with great admiration in Fargo during the winter or in New Orleans during the summer.

red-eye—A flight that operates overnight. *FA's symptom from one and the same.

roll-a-bag—Bag with wheels and a handle. *Bag that will most likely not fit under the seat.

second officer—Third pilot in charge, usually navigates the aircraft. *Pilot who does most of the work but gets the least pay.

service animal—A professionally trained animal that aids a person with a disability. *Usually better behaved than our two-legged passengers.

sick-bag—A bag located in your seat pocket that can be used for regurgitation. *A bag (hopefully) located in your seat pocket used for quick disposal of ingested airplane meals.

special meal—A meal that fits passengers' specific dietary or medical needs. Ordered when they make their reservation. *Maintains a quality level even lower than the normal airline meal.

Steve Slater—Flight attendant for JetBlue who reached his "stew" breaking point on August 9, 2010. *Has been grounded since yet remains a sky legend and a hero to some flight attendants.

stewardess—No such word. *No such word.

taxi—A verb describing the airplane's movement as it moves into position for take-off or arrival at the gate. *A time when many passengers decide to use the bathroom.

terminal—A noun defining the airport's building structure. *More appropriately defined in the dictionary as an adjective meaning "the end" or "fatal." To an FA it means the end if her arrival there is at the conclusion of her workday. But could be defined as fatally boring if she remains there for many hours in the middle of her workday. (This is referred to as "a sit".)

through flight—What your direct flight is called after it makes an intermediate stop. *Before which there is time to check out the cherry jam in the Grand Rapids airport.

trip—The duration of time between check-in and check-out time for an FA. Could be one to many days. *Duration not written in stone.

TSA—The Salvation Army, Tax Sheltered Annuity or, in this case, Transportation Security Administration. An airport security employee who works under the US Dept. of Homeland Security. *Makes a flight attendant's job safer and handles more "packages" than UPS.

unaccompanied minor—Any child traveling alone, for whom a fee has been paid for escort on and off flights. *The child kicking your seatback.

upgrade—Process through which a coach passenger is moved into first-class. *Process through which an FA could make extra money.

The **99** *Ways*

1. Believe that a reservation guarantees you a seat on an airplane

2. Board the airplane hungry

3. Don't know the FARS

4. Come unprepared

5. If you plan on happy hour, don't bring a credit card

6. Board the aircraft intoxicated

7. Ask for two predeparture drinks

8 Don't dress for the occasion

9. Don't bring treats for you flight attendants

10. Block the aisle during boarding

11. Be demanding as soon as you step foot on the airplane

12. Ask a flight attendant to stow your luggage

13. Believe that bulkhead seats are exempt from bag stowage rules

14. Believe that you bought an overhead bin with your ticket

15. Board the aircraft with 3 bags and the kitchen sink

16. Don't stow your bag properly

17. Refuse to check your bag

18. Expect to hang your garment bag in a coat closet

19. Send your six-year-old on a flight by himself

20. Be clueless to electronic device regulation

21. Use the bathroom while we are taxiing

22. Ask to be seated in first class

23. Refuse to follow crew instructions

24. Blame us for the weather

25. Try to obtain anything that is free

26. Be arrogant

27. Ask stupid questions

28. Tell stupid jokes

29. Believe that every airline and every aircraft is the same

30. Make physical contact with a flight attendant

31. Sit in a flight attendant's jumpseat

32. Take a newspaper or magazine from our jumpseat or luggage

33. Be impatient

34. Complain that you waited too long for service and then be unable to decide what you want

35. Tell a flight attendant she looks tired

36. Tell a flight attendant to smile

37. Pretend you have a personal servant

38. Pretend you don't speak English

39. Ring your call button often

40. Pretend that the plane is a restaurant

41. Have all your body parts and possessions in the aisle

42. Ignore us

43. Use the first-class bins or bathrooms when you are seated in coach

44. Roll your eyes if we don't have root beer

45. Contaminate our carts

46. Do not place your tray table down when we reach your row

47. Have your computer on the tray table when we are trying to place a meal there

48. Have your newspaper blocking our reach to the window seat passenger

49. Wallow in pity if we forget your row

50. Hang around the galley

51. Mumble when giving us your drink order

52. Ask for an extra meal

53. Order a special meal and don't claim it

54. See how many times you can make us run to the galley

55. Get upset when you don't get a meal choice

56. Complain about the meals

57. Parents, don't discuss with Junior his beverage choice before the cart gets to your row

58. Parents, don't be award that your kids will kick the seatback in front of them

59. Parents, be helpless

60. Believe that toddlers can safely bounce off the ceiling

61. Hand us a dirty diaper

62. Parents, don't be the adult

63. Passengers without kids, don't be an adult

64. Walk barefoot or let your child walk barefoot on an airplane

65. Forget your manners

66. Don't listen to the announcements

67. Joke about carrying a bomb or weapon

68. Try to take over the aircraft

69. Use the word "crash" in your speech

70. Call your flight attendant a "stewardess"

71. Take it out on us when the airline loses your bag or charges too much for your ticket

72. Believe that you'll receive a free ticket or first-class seat if you complain enough

73. Call your flight attendant names

74. Verbally abuse your flight attendant

75. Physically abuse your flight attendant

76. Make lewd comments to your flight attendant

77. Believe that being a flight attendant is glamorous

78. Have your priorities in the wrong order

79. Ask us to call ahead to hold your connecting flight

80. Assume all male flight attendants are gay

81. Venture to join the mile-high club

82. Pretend that you aren't in the old US of A

83. Believe that flight attendants have super powers

84. Use sign language when needing attention

85. Claim that your poodle is a service animal

86. Take your pet out of its carrier during the flight

87. Smoke in the bathrooms or anywhere near the airplane

88. If you're a doctor, nurse or EMT, don't respond to a medical emergency

89. Beat your neighbor to the aisle before the aircraft arrives at the gate

90. Be the first one out of your seat if you move slower than a snail

91. Strive to be the last one off the airplane

92. Believe that a "direct" flight will not stop in Denver or Miami

93. Stay on the airplane when on a "through" flight

94. Leave a mess

95. Take someone else's wheelchair

96. Order a wheelchair and then don't claim it

97. Take 57 snapshots of Junior in the cockpit when we're done deplaning

98. Ask a flight attendant in the gate area for directions as you deplane

99. Take yourself too seriously

Award-Winning Author
JoAnn Kuzma Deveny

An "iron ore miner's daughter," JoAnn Kuzma Deveny was born and raised on the Iron Range in northern Minnesota. She obtained a liberal arts degree at the University of Minnesota. To her father's dismay, JoAnn put her psychology degree to use on a flight attendant profession.

JoAnn has appeared on Fox National News, Rudy Maxa's World, KQRS Morning Show, KTIS 98.5 commenting on her humorous air travel book *99 Ways to Make a Flight Attendant Fly—Off the Handle!* and her inspirational memoir, *When Bluebirds Fly: Losing a Child, Living with Hope.* Her books have appeared in US News & World Report, Parenting Magazine, and other periodicals. Her third book, *I Am Widow, Hear Me Roar* was released in October 2018.

JoAnn continues her flying career and resides in Mound, Minnesota, where she is an accompanist for church services.

To order the newest revisions of JoAnn's books, please visit:

www.joanndeveny.com
or Amazon.com

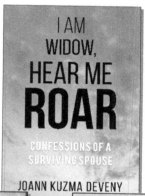

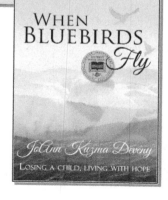